A Time for

SINGING

A HOW ANIMALS LIVE Book

A Time for

SINGING

Ron Hirschi

PHOTOGRAPHS BY *Thomas D. Mangelsen*

COBBLEHILL BOOKS/Dutton

For Ann Shotwell
—R. H.

For the children of Nebraska
—T. M.

Library of Congress Cataloging-in-Publication Data

Hirschi, Ron.
    A time for singing / Ron Hirschi ; photographs by Thomas D.
Mangelsen.
        p.   cm. —(A How animals live book)
    ISBN 0-525-65096-2
    1. Animal sounds—Juvenile literature.   [1. Animal sounds.]
I. Mangelsen, Thomas D., ill.   II. Title.   III. Series.
QL765.H65   1994
591.59—dc20   93-36772   CIP   AC

Published in the United States by Cobblehill Books,
an affiliate of Dutton Children's Books, a division of
Penguin Books USA Inc., 375 Hudson Street, New York, New York 10014
Designed by Charlotte Staub
Printed in Hong Kong
First Edition 10 9 8 7 6 5 4 3 2 1

Western meadowlark

Outside my window, meadowlarks
sing in the day's first light.
Beaks pointed to the sky, they
seem to call the sun to
brighten this new day.

Warblers of many kinds
join the springtime singing.
But do these tiny birds
sing just to wake you
from your sleep?

Yellow warbler

Marsh wren

Warblers, wrens,
and sparrows sing
songs their relatives
all remember

and you can learn
to name them all
if you listen
closely.

Vesper sparrow

Mountain bluebird

Bluebirds seem to say, "What cheer! What cheer!"
The bright blue males sing all alone,
calling their mates to inspect
nesting places.

Bohemian waxwings

Waxwings sing alone and in flocks,
even on the coldest winter day.

You can hear them call,
keeping track of one another,
as they search for berries
in the snow.

Bohemian and cedar waxwings

Cranes sing when they dance
the crane dance of spring.
Leaping and flapping, they clack long bills.

Then a female stands in silence.
A male circles, searching the ground
as if for just the right present.

Sandhill cranes dancing

He plucks a stone and tosses it high
into the air. And when he sings,
you can hear his voice all
up and down his very own valley.

Sandhill crane

Bald eagle

Eagles pierce the sky with
echoing screams that warn mates
and young ones when danger is near.

They seem to screech at you
and me, if we don't listen
to that warning.

Bald eagles

Common loon

In the calm morning air, loons call
with a song telling others not to come near.

Their beautiful song is meant for other loons,
helping a pair to claim a lake or
nesting place all their own.

Whales sing beneath the waves,
out in the deepest seas.

When they dive,
the orcas sing a song like no others.
Family members answer one another,
keeping track as they swim along shorelines
where many people listen too.
Someday, there is hope, we
might answer back in a
voice of understanding.

Orcas

Walrus dive down into
the darkest northern seas.

Just like the whale,
they sing to one another.

Females are almost silent,
but males ring, tap, and knock
with sounds that mingle with fish music
beneath the pounding surf.

Walrus

Seals sing.

Harbor seal

Tern colony

Shorebirds sing.

And fish sing too.
Fish songs are often clicking sounds,
quiet and low, far below.

Pacific herring

They sing just as we sing,
to communicate all that matters.
Songs are for survival, for company,
and for calling only those closest
to stay near.

Far above the clouds
in mountain valleys of the West,
you might hear the most piercing calls
you will ever hear.

On crisp autumn days the bugle of the elk
shatters the silence with a steaming, haunting call.
Bull elk sing to gather mates.
They also call out in warning
to their rivals.

Elk

In these same valleys,
listen overhead for the trumpet of the swans.

Trumpeters call to family,
gathering together as they search and search
for safe places to feed, sleep,
and to find warmth.

Trumpeter swans

Coyote sings in the morning or
just as the sun goes down.
Listen for coyote voices as the
wild dogs keep track of one another.

Join in that call
and just like your own pet,
the coyotes might understand
some of what you sing.

Sing with the animals.
Sing with the whispering wind.
There is always a time for singing
and a time just to listen to the
rest of our world.
What are the animals singing?
What do they say?
Maybe you will be the one
to find these answers
some day.

Afterword

The song of birds has long been used to help us tell one kind from another. Each bird has a voice like no other, so we can learn to recognize different species by listening closely. But the birds also sing differently throughout the year, so much so that people have also used the voice of birds to tell the season. One example is that described by Pretty Shield, a Crow woman who told of how the changes of the season were clearly spoken by a tiny chickadee. Pretty Shield said that the tongue of the chickadee changed throughout the year. Listen. These birds will call and sing with changing voice even though they almost always call out their name as well.

We actually know very little about animal language, even though we know they use voices to warn, attract, and establish territories. Whales, seals, and other marine animals, including fish, all have distinctive voices. We now know that individuals also sing with a unique voice. Scientists are now using that unique voice to track individuals, identifying song like a fingerprint. What the future might bring includes an ability to translate animal voices just like translating a human language different from our own. If you are like me, you probably speak to your pets. They can understand. But wouldn't it be wonderful if we really could speak to all animals with a voice of understanding!